SO-EFN-664

Books and Games

Bernard J. Weiss
Reading and Linguistics

Susan B. Cruikshank
Reading and Language Arts

Eldonna L. Evertts
Language Arts

Loreli Olson Steuer
Reading and Linguistics

Janet Sprout
Educational Consultant

Lyman C. Hunt
General Editor—Satellite Books

Holt
Basic
Reading

Level 4

HOLT, RINEHART AND WINSTON, PUBLISHERS
New York • Toronto • London • Sydney

Copyright © 1980, 1977, 1973 by Holt, Rinehart and Winston, Publishers
All Rights Reserved
Printed in the United States of America

ISBN 0-03-047766-2
  123   071   987654

Acknowledgments:

Grateful acknowledgment is given to the following authors and publishers:

McIntosh & Otis, for ''Picture People,'' from *Whispers and Other Poems.* Copyright © 1958 by Myra Cohn Livingston. Used by permission.

Highlights for Children, for ''My Dog,'' by Marguerite Hamilton from *Children's Activities.* Used by permission.

Instructor Publications, Inc., for ''Shopping,'' by Josephine van Dolzen Pease from *The Instructor.* Used by permission.

Art Credits:

Ray Cruz, pages 4 – 5
Eleanor Mill, pages 6 – 25, 27 – 34, 36 – 42, 44 – 61
Tien, page 26
Marilyn Bass Goldman, page 35
Jan Palmer, page 43
Lionel Kalish, pages 62 – 63
Cover art by James Endicott

Table of Contents

Picture People   *a poem by Myra Cohn Livingston*   5

A Game Book   6

Jenny and Jay Cook   16

Candy   *a recipe*   24

LANGUAGE: Making Words   26

Rex   27

My Dog   *a poem by Marguerite Hamilton*   35

The Cookie Store   36

LANGUAGE: Stringing Words   43

Find the Cookies   44

The Big Store   54

Shopping   *a poem by Josephine van Dolzen Pease*   62

NEW WORDS   64

Picture People

I like to peek

inside a book

where all the picture people look.

I like to peek

at them and see

if they are peeking back at me.

—Myra Cohn Livingston

A Game Book

Jim has a game book.

Jim reads the book.

Jim sees a game for one.

Jim plays the game.

Jim likes the game for one.

The game book helps Jim.

Don comes into the house.

Don and Jim read the game book.

The boys see a game for two.

The two boys play the game.

The boys play the game for two.

The boys like the game.

Meg comes into the house.

Meg and Don and Jim read the book.

They see a game for three.

Meg and Don and Jim play the game.

They play the game for three.

They like the game for three.

Meg says, "Good-by."

Don and Jim play a game.
They play the game for two.

Don says, "Good-by."

14

Jim plays a game.

Jim plays the game for one.

Jim has fun.

Jenny and Jay Cook

Meg and Jenny and Jay are in the house.

Meg is big.

Jenny and Jay are little.

Meg and Jay see a book.

They look in the book.

Meg reads the book.

Meg reads the book to Jay.

17

Jenny sees cookies in the book.

Jenny likes cookies.

Meg and Jay like cookies.

Meg reads the book.

Jenny and Jay make the cookies.

They make the cookies in the book.

The cookies go in.

20

And the cookies come out.
The cookies are not good.

21

The cookies go in.

And the cookies come out.

The cookies look good.

The cookies are good!

Jenny and Jay and Meg make good cookies.

They are good cooks!

Candy

Make some peanut butter candy.

You need

    1 cup peanut butter

    1 cup corn syrup

    1¼ cups powdered milk

    1¼ cups powdered sugar

First mix it.

Roll it into little balls.

Then eat one.

Making Words

Initial Consonant Substitution. Have the first word read. Point out that the girl is changing the first letter. Have the new word read. Continue with the remaining words.

Rex

"Here, Rex," said Don.

"Come here.

Come and see the dog book."

"Here is a good trick," said Don.

"Come and see the trick.

Come out here, Rex.

Do the trick!"

Rex did come out.

Rex did not do the trick.

"Come here, Rex!
Good dog," said Don.
"Do the trick!"

Rex did not do the trick.

"Rex is not a trick dog," said Don.

"Come here.

Come into the house, Rex."

Rex did not go in.
Rex did the trick!

My Dog

My dog is lots of company
When I am all alone,
But he is too much company
When I have an ice cream cone!

—Marguerite Hamilton

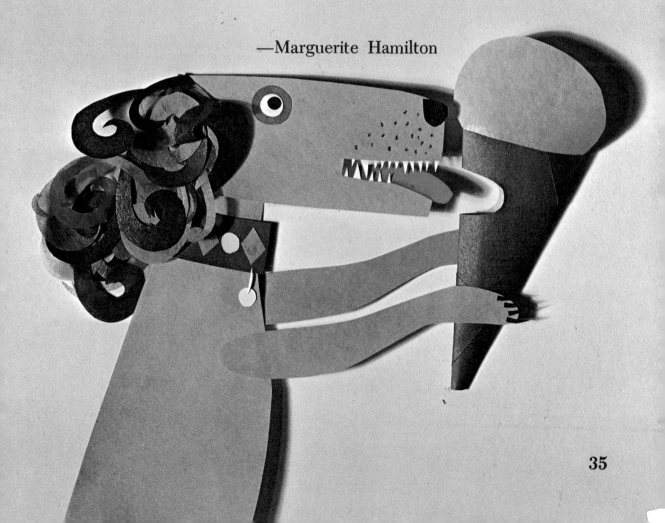

The Cookie Store

Meg and Rosa play.
They play store.

Meg and Rosa make a sign.
They make a big sign.
The sign says, "Cookie Store."

Cookies are in the store.

Jim sees the sign.

Jim goes into the store.

Jim sees big and little cookies.

The cookies look good.

One cookie looks like a bear.

One cookie looks like a pig.

Jim sees a big cookie.

The big cookie looks good.

The cookie looks like a little house.

"The little house is for me," says Jim.

Jim goes out.

Jenny sees the sign.

Jenny goes into the store.

She looks for a cookie.

She sees the pig cookie.

She sees the bear cookie.

"The pig is not for me," says Jenny.

"The bear is not for me."

Jenny sees the cookie she likes.

The cookie is a little dog.

"The little dog is for me," says Jenny.

Jenny goes out.

Here comes Rex.

Rex goes into the store.

Rex sees the cookies.

Rex likes the cookies.

"Go out, Rex," says Meg.

"The store is not for a dog," says Rosa.

"The cookies are not for Rex."

Rex goes for the cookies.

Down come the cookies!
Down comes the sign!
Down comes the store!

Good-by, cookies and sign!
Good-by, store!

Stringing Words

The	boy	makes	games.
A	girl	sees	cookies.
One	bear	likes	books.

The	boys	make	games.
Two	girls	see	cookies.
Three	bears	like	books.

Sentence Patterns. Have the children choose a word from each column to form sentences.

Find the Cookies

The boys and girls play a game.

They play "Find the Cookies."

They see a big sign on a house.

Bob reads the sign.

The sign says, "Go into the house."

Go into the house.

45

The boys and girls go into the house.

The boys and girls see a little sign.

They read the little sign.

The sign says, "Find Rex."

The boys and girls find Rex.

Pat sees a sign on Rex.

She reads the sign.

The sign says, "Find a blue book."

The boys and girls see the books.

"Here is the blue book," says Bob.

"A sign is in the book."

Pat reads the sign.

The sign says, "Find a big book."

Jenny sees the big book.

She sees a sign in the book.

Don reads the sign.

The sign says, "Find a blue pig."

"A blue pig!" says Jenny.

"Come in here," says Jim.

"Here is a blue pig.

Come and see the pig."

The boys and girls see the pig.

They do not see a sign on the pig.

They do not see cookies.

The boys and girls look and look.
They look in the blue pig.

Here are the cookies.

The cookies are **in** the blue pig!

The Big Store

Three boys go to the big store.

They go to find books.

The boys see two signs.

Bob reads the In sign.

Don and Bob go in.

Jim sees the Out sign.

Jim goes in.

"Read the signs, Jim," says Don.

"The sign is the Out sign.

Find the In sign and go in."

The boys are in the store.

They see two signs.

One sign says, "Up."

One sign says, "Down."

Bob and Don go up.

And Jim goes down.

"Come here, Jim," says Don.

"The books are up here.

Read the signs.

Find the Up sign and come up."

Jim sees the Up sign.

Jim goes up.

The three boys find the books.

They see the Down sign.

Bob goes down.

Don goes down.

And Jim goes down.

The three boys see the Out sign.

Bob goes out.

Don goes out.

And Jim goes out.

Shopping

I like to hop,
    and I like to skip,
And I like to go
    on a shopping trip.

I like to stand
    by the bookman's shelf
And choose a book
    all by myself.

—Josephine van Dolzen Pease

New Words

The words listed beside the page numbers below are introduced in *Books and Games,* Level 4 in the HOLT BASIC READING SERIES. The words printed in italics are easily decoded.

6. game	21. *not*	sign
8. *comes*	*good*	37. goes
into	out	38. me
read	27. here	39. she
boys	*Rex*	42. down
9. *like*	said	44. find
10. they	dog	girls
12. says	29. trick	*on*
16. Jenny	*do*	47. blue
Jay	30. *did*	55. *signs*
18. cookies	36. Rosa	57. *up*
19. make	*cookie*	
20. go	store	